Seasons
of
Grace

Other Books by Mark A. Noll

Adding Cross to Crown: The Political Significance of Christ's Passion

Amazing Grace: Evangelicalism in Australia, Britain, Canada, and the United States (editor, with George Rawlyk)

Between Faith & Criticism: Evangelicals, Scholarship, and the Bible in America

The Bible in America: Essays in Cultural History (editor, with Nathan Hatch)

Charles Hodge: The Way of Life (editor)

Christian Faith and Practice in the Modern World: Theology from an Evangelical Point of View (editor, with David Wells)

Christians and the American Revolution

Confessions and Catechisms of the Reformation (editor)

Eerdmans' Handbook to Christianity in America (editor, with Nathan Hatch, George Marsden, David Wells, and John Woodbridge)

Evangelicalism: Comparative Studies of Popular Protestantism in North America, the British Isles, and Beyond, 1700–1900 (editor, with George Rawlyk and David Bebbington)

The Gospel in America: Themes in the Story of America's Evangelicals (with John Woodbridge and Nathan Hatch)

A History of Christianity in the United States and Canada

One Nation under God? Christian Faith and Political Action in America

Princeton and the Republic, 1768–1822: The Search for a Christian Enlightenment in the Era of Samuel Stanhope Smith

The Princeton Defense of Plenary Verbal Inspiration (editor)

The Princeton Theology, 1812–1921: Scripture, Science, and Theological Method from Archibald Alexander to Benjamin Breckinridge Warfield (editor)

Religion and American Politics: From the Colonial Period to the 1980s (editor)

The Scandal of the Evangelical Mind

The Search for Christian America (with Nathan Hatch and George Marsden)

Voices from the Heart: Four Centuries of American Piety (editor, with Roger Lundin)

What Is Darwinism? And Other Writings on Science and Religion, by Charles Hodge (editor, with David Livingstone)

Seasons
of
Grace

Mark A. Noll

Baker Books
A Division of Baker Book House Co.
Grand Rapids, Michigan 49516

Library of Congress Cataloging-in-Publication Data

Noll, Mark A., 1946–
    Seasons of grace / Mark A. Noll.
      p   cm.
    ISBN 0-8010-5777-9 (pbk.)
    1. Grace (Theology)—Poetry. I. Title.
PS3564.042S4 1997
811'.54—dc21   97-19619

Some of the poems in this book first appeared, often in earlier versions, in the following publications:

Christianity Today: "Hymn to God on My Way to Him" (July 3, 1970); "And the Word Was Made Flesh" (Dec. 4, 1970); "Quickening" (March 31, 1972); "The Gospel According to Ruth" (Dec. 7, 1973).

HIS: "Christ's Crown" (April 1979).

The Reformed Journal: "Ecce Agnus: At the Blood Bank on Good Friday" (April 1981); "In Time the Cross" (July 1985); "Performing Bach 1985" (Aug. 1985); "Longing Hearts" (Nov. 1985); "Three Abstractions for Advent" (Dec. 1987); "Born to Raise the Sons of Earth" (Dec. 1987); "Sing, Choirs of Angels" (Dec. 1988); "Evensong, King's College Chapel" (April 1989); "Scots' Form in the Suburbs" (Nov. 1989); "Nunc Dimittis (December 26, 1989)—Romania" (Jan. 1990).

The Cresset: "The Widow of Zarephath" (May 1984) [now titled: "But the Lord Was Not in the Wind"]; "At the Sacrament, Late January in Chicago" (Jan. 1987).

New Oxford Review: "J. S. Bach: In Memoriam, 1685–1750" (June 1984).

A Widening Light: Poems of the Incarnation, ed. Luci Shaw (Wheaton: Harold Shaw, 1984): "Et Resurrexit Tertia Die."

Cross Currents: "Verba Verbumque: Hus at Constance" (Spring 1993).

First Things: "Cold Dawn at the Shelter" (Dec. 1993).

For information about academic books, resources for Christian leaders, and all new releases available from Baker Book House, visit our web site:
http://www.bakerbooks.com

To
our family in God
at Immanuel Presbyterian Church

The shepherds sing; and shall I silent be?
My God, no hymne for thee?
My soul's a shepherd too; a flock it feeds
Of thoughts, and words, and deeds.
The pasture is thy word: the streams, thy grace
Enriching all the place.
Shepherd and flock shall sing, and all my powers
Out-sing the day-light houres.
—George Herbert

Contents

Preface   9

J. S. Bach
Performing Bach 1985   *12*
Et Resurrexit Tertia Die   *13*
In Memoriam, 1685–1750   *14*
Jesu schläft, was soll ich hoffen   *16*

Advent
Born to Raise the Sons of Earth   *18*
Three Abstractions for Advent   *19*
Advent 1989 Romania   *20*
Longing Hearts   *22*
Surprise!   *24*
And the Word Was Made Flesh   *25*
Sing, Choirs of Angels   *26*
Mid-Life Christmas   *28*
Advent Communion   *29*
The Gospel According to Ruth   *30*

Passion
Ecce Agnus: At the Blood Bank on Good Friday   *38*
Christ's Crown   *40*
In Time the Cross   *41*
Easter Litany   *42*
Quickening   *43*

Mighty Acts of God
The Creation of Man   *46*
Hymn to God on My Way to Him   *47*
The Lion and the Lamb   *48*
The Sensitive Nostrils of God   *50*
Snow   *51*
Scots' Form in the Suburbs   *52*
At the Sacrament, Late January in Chicago   *54*

The Domestic Round

for her birthday in almost Spring 56
A Mother Muses on Receiving the Kingdom
    of Heaven as a Child 57
A Hymn to Marriage, Plena Gratia, after Ten Years 58
"But the Lord Was Not in the Wind" 59
Advent Journey to a Recent Widower 60
Evensong, King's College Chapel 61
Memorial Quartet 62
For Mary, on Graduating from College 65

Texts/Sermons

Advent Meditation on Psalm 119:25, 28, 31 68
Behold, I Stand at the Door 70
The Storm 71
Meditation for a Christmas Communion 72
Philippian Jailer 74

Friends

Lament from Ely Cathedral for
    Sheri Nystrom Scandrett, 1966–1988 76
Pastor Harvey Marks a Decade with
    His Congregation 78
To Bob and JoAnn Harvey 80
To Arthur Holmes, on His Retirement 81
A Historian's History, 1939–1989 82
Cold Dawn at the Shelter 84
Casting Christmas 1994 85
Big George 86

Times Past

Verba Verbumque: Hus at Constance 88
Stalingrad: Even a Soldier Is the City of God 89
Martyrdom (for the Rev. Robert Ziemer) 90
In Rama Sat Rachel Weeping, with Wilfred
    Her Husband 92
Election 1968 95

Preface

The poems in this book are intended to mean something, not just *be*. They come from one life's experiences and were inspired especially by the people who have given meaning to that life and by the God to whom that life has been drawn. Because these poems do not pretend to stand on their own, it may help to know a little about the people who have done the most to bring them into existence. Maggie Packer was born in New Jersey on March 20, 1947, one day short of the 262nd birthday of Johann Sebastian Bach. I met her in January or February 1967 during a class on medieval English literature at Wheaton College. We were married December 27, 1969. Mary Constance Noll was born on Christmas day, 1973; David Luther Noll, two days short of Epiphany, 1978; Robert Francis Noll, who is named for his grandfathers, on September 9, 1984.

J. S. Bach

Performing Bach 1985

Tonight we hear you, old Johann
Sebastian, pure, sublime—as near as man,
and this time woman singing too,
could come to what your genius conceived,
your artful hand inscribed, but you

      had never heard yourself. Not this time boys
      with middling skill and wandering eye
      or sleepy burghers bored by "irksome noise."

Our leads, with seconds standing by,
were world class, our instruments as *echt*
as yours, our hall acoustically
precise, our stage well lit, our seats designed

      for ease. We had no choirs resigned
      to rushed rehearsals, strained artistically
      as amateurs and drawn piecemeal
      from every class among the *Volk.*

And in our programs was a well-
phrased treatise on the pleasures of Baroque
for study at the interval

      instead of gospel readings, ancient rites,
      and sermons—plain continuo
      of words to ground the unalloyed delights
      that poured forth with an artless art
      from deep within your craftsman's praising heart.

Et Resurrexit Tertia Die
(B-Minor Mass)

Three short days of twilight and darkness,
dawn and the light. The elements, free from
all knowledge, unblessed by prediction, yet sensed the
      suspense—
Creator entombed by creation, the loftiest heights
brought low, the universe madly askew. Three
short days with the length of three endless nights.

Three times, forced by its nature to shine,
the sun reluctantly rose. In the skies no sign
through clouds of a bow. The earth which knew not
      how sinless
its Maker turned Captive had been yet felt the wrong.
The wind whistled dirges. Three endless
days—then the groan of creation exploded in song.

In Memoriam, 1685-1750

"Bach is my best friend.
He is the God of music."
                    —Pablo Casals

Oh, rejoice to imagine the scene up above
midst the jamming that brightens the mansions of love
at the midpoint along in the Century of Light
with the host at full voice—the innumerable throng
with their bellow and bray for the Lamb-from-the-dead,
        and the much smaller band for whom song
        is an art, as the word quickly spread,

        "Old Bach is here!"

The former monk is first to grasp his hand.
Then family gathers round, with some reserve,
but other countrymen fly out pell-mell,
an echo of the watchman's voice. Johan
and Paul, Philip, Dietrich Buxtehude,
and one brisk hug from Silberman. Then soon
above their heads he spies the circle of
the Roman South: Great Gregory, Ambrose,
with Giovanni and Antonio.
His eyes light up, reflecting no surprise;
he shouts—in middling Latin—starts of course
to hum. The din expands, it surges like
the waves on Galilee until his lips
begin to move—Shh, ahh, the master speaks.

And once again he whispers as he had
in such profuse magnificence before:

> "Jesus help me. God alone be praised."

The song resumes. At first it sounds
the same, but soon its peaks stretch higher.
Chorales and preludes, masses, rounds,
cantatas, fugues strike brighter fire
in Cross-drawn counterpoint. Thus those
with skill. The rest, the milling mass of sheep,
add bleat, with joy, to ever safer bleat.

Jesu schläft, was soll ich hoffen

("Jesus sleeps, what hope have I?"—
The opening aria from Cantata No. 81
for the Fourth Sunday after Epiphany)

I was late. (even) The rain beat my face.
Would they, could they understand? My coat wouldn't do.
(even) My suit would be wet. The car—no space
to park it at all. (even the wind) I knew
it was useless; and yet I rushed on until
from somewhere He appeared—no let up of rain,
the cars slithered by, the air was filled
with care, with cares, the teeming of my brain—
He was walking beside me now (even the wind,
even the wind and the sea), He grabbed me and shook me.
"I'm late, can't You see," I screamed—it was cold; the din
overwhelmed me, I could barely see—
the rain blasting down. He called me clear, converted my
     choice:
"Even the wind and the sea obey my voice."

Advent

Born to Raise the Sons of Earth

I am busy, Jesus,
screeching ever faster round and round—
you lie calmly in the manger,
Joseph's patient voice the only sound.

I am selfish, Jesus,
grasping, pulling inward, curved in tight—
you stoop lower, ever lower,
mixing spittle for a poor man's sight.

I am sated, Jesus,
stuffed so full I've almost lost my breath—
you are rasping, breathing labored,
stumbling naked, famished, to your death.

I am tired, Jesus,
numb and finished, callous and depressed—
you stand wounded, weeping, dying,
quickened; calling, come to me and rest.

Three Abstractions for Advent

Transcendence

A subtle irony of our new age
of darkness lies in this, that great
Sir Isaac Newton, maker of our world,
read Scripture year by year by year to date
the End of Time and thereby almost saw
that formulae were only able to define
the whirling mass because the Lord had made
the merest inclination of his mind.

Immanence

While Joseph had enough to do
to tend the fire and keep
the stock preoccupied so both
his wife and child could sleep,
he still could think about himself,
the years to come, the plight
of age relieved by this new life
who whimpered in the night.

Mystery

On Christmas Eve as candles feebly calm
the neon glare, a minister breaks bread
for worshippers whose worn, tumultuous hearts
hang on the ancient words that have been said
in just this way time without end, as if
this nourishment, this crumb, this drop contained
the universe, the last shalom, the only
truth that cannot be explained.

Advent 1989 Romania

Magnificat (December 12)

When Christian brothers gather with their wives
and children this year in Romania
to read the Christmas story, they will hear
as well, because they watch Hungarian
TV and listen to the BBC,
the thudding sound of rulers falling from
their thrones, of proud men scattered in their own
imaginings, and they will pray, how long,
O Lord, how long?

                    In cities spread throughout
the West their friends, who gape with wonder on
the ruins of an iron curtain, pray
two prayers: O Lord, for them, how long? For us,
the rich, are we the ones you send away
with nothing?
                  God responds as earlier
he had replied to other men of might
and other outcasts strewn through times of want,
of bondage, or rare fleeting moments of
repose. Heed humble Mary lifted high
who shows to free and bound the way: her child
is bread where lines are long at Peoples' Co-
ops and where bulging shelves cannot contain
the huge supply, his words are life alike
where there are far too many books and where
the book of books is banned, this mercy born

in Bethlehem to those who fear his name,
to far-flung heirs of Abraham, survives,
protects, revives, inspires, directs, delights,
engulfs the bliss-bound circling of the years.

Nunc Dimittis (December 26)

Old Simeon, who waited patiently
to see the consolation promised long
before, dwelt much upon the Spirit of
the Lord, who in this child would be a sign
of contradiction, vainly flailed against
and ever laying bare the hidden thoughts
of prideful hearts, a sign to cause the rise
and fall of many.
              Many fall. They sing
this year with joy unspeakable the songs
of Christmas in the streets of Bucharest
and shield their eyes beyond belief against
a piercing light for revelation to
the Gentiles.
           Yet beyond the carols from
Romania another theme is heard
this surging Christmastide of questions: will
another tyrant—race, chaos, or greed—
replace the fallen? What remains from such
a night of terror for the dawning? Who
will be the Spirit's witness of the Child
to bind the wounds, mop up the tears, and draw
the piercing sword from Timisoara's soul?

Longing Hearts

The lines are long, the lot is full,
my son's impatient to attack the tree.
At Advent though the time grows short,
the hours creep by. Strange grace—that waiting, dull
and blank, unmasks reality.

    The waiting for the court's decree
    is cruel. The family's torn, their friends have fled.
    And they, eyes dimmed as week gives way
    to paralyzing week, begin to see
    the black suspense that lies ahead.

    The waiting in a parent's room
    is cold, where children, filled with loving care,
    yet pray confused. Exhausted, spent,
    they struggle through an antiseptic gloom
    like toddlers on an endless stair.

    The waiting for the morning mail
    is tense if destinies depend upon
    the letters that come back. Though all
    unseen, they weave our story, tell our tale,
    define a future still unknown.

    The waiting through a full nine months
    is long—or so it seems. Once past, the heart
    exults, but then is sobered by
    the real span of waiting that confronts
    the parents who have made this start.

And so at Advent and throughout
the year we wait. The eye of hope would dim,
the years slide by with numbing force,
faith pass from patient certainty to doubt
to death, did not an angel's hymn
once call cold shepherds waiting in
the dark to seek a Healer-Brother-Friend,
did not a holy baby wait
no longer to embrace the scourge of sin
and point our waiting to its end.

Surprise!

Now almost thirty years ago, the shock
of swiftly sliding moods remains as fresh
as yesterday—first anger (I am turned
eighteen and am a god—no merely mortal
parents can keep me at home when I
would prowling go) and then chagrin (so, why
are Patrick, Dave and Dennis, Ron and Tom,
and Jim arriving all at once?) and last
mute wonder at a lifetime's covenant
from mother and from father of such love.

    The second time was just eight weeks
    ago—no anger now but dazed
    incomprehension (why on such
    a night to drive so far?) dispatched
    by deep humility (for just
    this book? for me?) and then delight
    to find in one small space so many
    of the friends I love the most.

        Such gifts—and twice in one
        short life, are mysteries
        of which the only source
        could be the unawaited
        love that once surprised
        us all at Bethlehem.

And the Word Was Made Flesh

Before the jingle bells
the Jesus boy—
and Christ (in vain the fundamental certainty)
has not been slain upon an Xmas tree.
But incognito (like an insect drawn to flame),
as being found with human hells as man,
in being flesh—saved flesh
and mistletoe and wassailing joy
(and saved the jingle bells).

Sing, Choirs of Angels

Did shepherds catch in angels' song
a symphony announced among
the fleeting notes of more than earthly praise? And
did they hear those voices as the prelude to a vast
polyphony, a surging oratorio for instruments from every
    land
and tribe and tongue?

A piece so grand it could inspire with excess undiminished
        singing popes and Martin Luther's lullaby,
            the very thought of St. Bernard and Charles Wesley's
                interest in the Savior's blood,
        Messiah's choreographer, the organist of Leipzig,
        and a noble choir of latter-day Elijahs—
        Routley, Clarkson, Messiaen—
        singing, singing with the knee unbowed.

A theme so large it swallows up the blast
        of trumpets, wail of bagpipes, drummers drumming as
            to war,
        the most exalted and the most pathetic
        dirges, requiems, laments,
        cacophony of wailers, snorters, gulpers, wheezers
            making melodié to the Lord.

A work so bold it would sustain
     the warbling notes of children,
     tiny crusaders who lisped feeble hymns to their doom,
     and clear soprano voices fine enough to pierce a heart of
          stone,
     David picking out O Come, O Come Emmanuel,
     Mary piping, piping on a fragile reed,
     Robert stumbling on the words of Precious Jewels,
          Precious Jewels.

When the silence of the ages was rent
with a song, did the shepherds take heed
of the compass, the sweep, the extent
of what took place as God resolved to bend
his bow crescendoing in time and send
his pealing voice through ages without end?

Mid-Life Christmas

November and December strike
a dull, uncertain sound, so full so fast
the world spins, more trouble than it's worth
for Thanks to clot the year-end dash
without the added complication of
    a Savior's birth.

So many friendly voices raised—
read this write that go here teach there; such all-
consuming energies required at hearth
and home; however eager pall
of self remains. What space is left to contemplate
    a Savior's birth?

The mystery is by adding more
to clear a way, to rise (as years churn by
borne down, filled flush, clogged full) with earth-
bound flesh, to hear a single feeble cry
so clear amid disharmony announce
    a Savior's birth.

Advent Communion

"We invite you to carry the communion hymn insert with you
as you approach the table."

Who can sing "When I Survey
the Wondrous Cross" with gentle chords
from calm guitar, discern the vast array
of real life our humble church affords
and know we know how deep
the depths of grief and wide the bounteous hand
of grace in just this room, and not understand
why we sit in our places and weep?

Music brings the dead almost
to life. "Almost" is what the tears
are for. We crave the Host because our host
is thinned. We sing "Amazing Grace" and years
evaporate, and keep
on singing as the melody distends
our hearts, so full are they filled with the faces of friends.
I am fifty years old and I weep.

Advent hymns are sharper still,
for they recall as well a tree
of light, great love, a warm domestic thrill
from years ago. With them we also see
a newborn child who sleeps
while Mary ponders loneliness, the blood,
the cold, and a doorway flung wide into glory and God.
By the manger she watches and weeps.

The Gospel According to Ruth

Narration: If, beyond the grave,
exist reflection, memory,
subjection to the craving
to recall a vanished history;
and if the lives beyond
all dying still may sense somehow the earth—
detached, pristine, not causing it—
ancestors of the Christ may
have been there, might have seen
the sight that night
when God enslaved himself by birth.

Winding out in whispers, spirits lurking
in the dank and dripping corners of the cave
breathe their wonder
at the Father's finally worded nave,
his gentle gauntlet flung down to the world.

In the chorus move the strains
of joy, of proud fulfillment, and of mortified
    chagrin—
all awed; but seeping somewhere in
the dry and faint remains
of weeping, weeping high and fine
from a strained and lonely face—
Orpah weeping for her almost own
that were not; tears for him, for them,
and most for Boaz whom she'd never known.

Orpah: My sister went with old Naomi when
           she left here, found herself once more a bride
           and took (in love) for her God their God. Then
           just as Naomi had, in peace, she died.
           Her curse upon herself, like gardens do
           when spread with dung, bloomed into life.
                 (Their God
           had always done this for the ones who knew
           how near he was to hear.) Her twilight held
           the joy of seeing their son's grandson who
           became both son and father of her God.
           They left me stripped of love and hope and all
           the promise I had spent in choices
           squandered then, but now beyond recall—
           abandoned, hearing only echoed voices . . .

Naomi: Come, men! Away from dust,
           away from parching ground, we
           must seek a new land, find
           some new blood, seek
           in rumored green and rivers some relief.

Elimelech: Though death detain me I will sing
           both leaving here and going where
           his light is dim what he did there
           in Egypt's dark. For he will bring
           into this stricken land respìte
           to those who sit without a light
           but sharp-eyed for the promised King.

Mahlon: Why, when there is now enough to eat
           do the harpies beat thus, bite thus
           deep within my throat?

31

Why then do the red flecks sparkle
in the sputum spat into the sunlight?
Where then is that Yahweh? Why, when in the
    sky
at last are clouds (that I'll admit are
pagan) do I have to die?

Chilion: There my brother (phaw! his rancid
innards succored death for me) can
see no further than his expectoration
or his nightly enema;
while we, expatriates from the Promised Land,
disport ourselves with dogs. Like Esau,
he was hungry, we were hungry, selling out our
rights of promise for a hunger we could not
    withstand.

Together: Come, wives, hold our heads of Promise
on your barren pagan wombs;
you may tell your sometime nieces, nephews
in your haggard days—you have known
    Jehovah's rods,
given them a decent tomb.

Elimelech: With this my last and cloying breath
I praise thee Lord. Now, come sweet death.

Naomi: So soon you're gone now, husband-lover,
strangely foreign sons of mine;
Pray God? yes, but where in rag-tag
foreign blood could ever be
another hope or any other man for me?

Orpah: And now the voices shriek out of the darkness:
            mine, Naomi's (who would say her name
            was Mara, bitterness) and Ruth's who in
            a whisper loud as icy thunder says
            she'll go as well. My last farewell mocks on.
            The voices rise from far away. Yet they
            are clearer now; like knives they pierce my ears.

Naomi: Now once more home.
            I bring one proven love away from there,
            one final solace for a death-dealt, God-forsaken
                crone.

Boaz: That Moab woman strikes my fancy;
            she is kin—Naomi's, mine—it's said.
            Perhaps the time to fill my empty bed
            is now; I'll search and see;
            the time for sons is almost by.

Narration: There is within the spirits' chorus
            (at the sight of him, the real new Jerusalem)
            one voice antiphonal to Orpah's
            keening for a lost and shriveled self—
            a voice, that had she too gone back,
            she would have known as next-of-kin.

Next-of-kin: I sold my damnèd rights of birth for . . .
            what? A fear of strangers,
            scent of danger?
            Scorn of neighbors, fear of favor
            lost because some pagan shares my bed?

The reasons why are so absurd
(they must have been) I can't remember when
before then
I had lost my awe of God and thought
to sound my soul by men.

Ruth: It was a daring gambit; she,
       Naomi, forced me to it; but though we faced
          despair,
       she knew that Israel's God delights
       in risks. And through it all Naomi clung
       to him. Now the child I bear
       will be hers too; the days and nights
       he dreams of God, her legacy; and if perhaps
          among
       his children's children comes the Father's
       promised One, then he will too belong to her.

Naomi: My life is now about to end.
       But in its dusk there is a dawn
       that nothing's sweeter than except
       the sweetness of my daughter's milk
       the baby feeds upon.

She alone who bore the Child
and nursed him at her breast
received as consummation what
was prayer for all the rest.

Those who bore the years before
the hour of holy birth
sustained through grief, remorse, and doubt
God's lineage on earth.

Root of Jesse! Royal heir
of David! Orpah's fear
is out of place, Naomi's hope,
the son of Ruth is here.

Praise the God who sent the Son
to solve time's mystery:
in Christ he found the lost and blessed
a faithful ancestry.

Praise the Father! Praise the Son
who sums up all, the last
of Adam's race: the hope of all,
both now and in the past.

Passion

Ecce Agnus:
At the Blood Bank on Good Friday

For Don Melton, August 20, 1938–December 31, 1973

The blood bank. Year of our Lord, nineteen
and seventy-one. As I went in
the oldest man I'd ever seen
slipped out. The spotless nurse, when asked,
had said he came to clean
his pipes out once each year. "Old goat!
This giving of blood is not what it seems."
She probed my finger, asked if I were
sick or had VD. I paled, felt caught between

claiming my oldest and most private right
to hoard all my fluids (the plasma is life!)
or baring my cold pale arm to the knife,
the needle that offered my blood for the fight
to hold back a dying man's impatient night.

"Just squeeze this little ball until
you're told to stop," she said
as dull black blood pulsed out to fill
the sack that'd lain as still
as death beside my arm. . . . The nurse
asked, "Who's it for (hold tight and we'll
be done, ahhh . . . there! in no time at all)?"
And I said, letting loose of the ball,
"for a man who has fallen incurably ill."

"How sad," she intoned as she dabbed at the red
blotch marking the place of the wound. The thread
was sustained as a chill like postpartum
and a throbbing like lancets encircled my head.

Christ's Crown

The leaves emerge—a growing
garland lying lightly on his head.
The dance of spring, of resurrection,
quicks his feet; from all directions
caper those he'll call his own.
The sun shines warming down upon
the dancers 'round their pivot. Only those
up close can smell or see the thick
black-red the flowers nurse upon.

In Time the Cross

Now glows the cross with blinding light
pulsating from a mushroom cloud—
within the cross the glare is dimmed,
drawn in, defeated, overawed
by Pillar of Shekinah bright.

Now stands the cross blood red, heaped high
with dying half-formed infants crushed—
within the cross their cries assume
the harmony of angels hushed
by Mary's manger lullaby.

Now fades the cross to drab, borne down
into the drudge of day on day—
within the cross the cruelest wood
is shaped for loftiest display
by care-worn carpentry profound.

Now sinks the cross, with darkness thronged,
into the barren void of death—
within the cross the night contracts,
pierced through at Easter's clean first breath
by Christ our Dayspring, Hope, and Dawn.

Easter Litany

The choir in the loft—earnest, attentive, and bright—
arose to sing a lush and sprightly song.
The oblation washed down and mingled with sunlight
that dappled the burnished pews and reflected along
row upon row of spring-like resplendence: green,
gold, blue, brisk browns and grays. Liveried
in style, the church presents itself, a clean,
fresh, fragrant savor on the day of its delivery.

Up high in front he hangs, stretched out and mauled
of trunk and limb; his face is smeared and gory,
his lips gape open, yet speechless, at a loss
for words once more to remind them all
before they are swept up in splendor and gone, that the
     glory
of the church is the blood-black scandal of the cross.

Quickening

Dead trees draw life
when the days expand and the sun
fulfills its promise, oft delayed
by the clutch of ice.

Clotted, gnarled, knotted twigs
on the trees sense sap and the death
of death. They stretch, begin
to puff green on the end.

We sing new songs
of a Life laid down for rebirth
when Easter is the Spring
and the branch is Christ.

Mighty Acts of God

The Creation of Man

The rookie, ready, strode to the plate—
his first time up.
There is great concern in the pit of his stomach.
He sees five pitches; they are good,
but still he waits. And then
on three and two
the change.

His body's out in front,
he's all but swung—
yet hanging, hanging, hanging back
as if to bring the cosmos up to him
till both were primed—
he's waiting, full of straining wrists and bracing arms
and legs (tipping his weight around).

He swings, and
CRACK! a ponderous shot curves slightly up and rises
like a trail of smoke.
The fielders all stand still. The drive
pellucid clear, rising, rising, going as no ball
from any bat has ever gone before:
rising like a sunbeam on its journey back—
going, going, going . . . FOUL!

He's standing at the plate,
his leaping heart sinks into sadness
as this quintessent curve of power goes astray,
watching, watching, watching still—
rookies always watch their fouls.

Hymn to God on My Way to Him

I sing of rumored splendor hiding some-
where far across a dried and fissured flood
of gray. Dead it seems. My search
like climbing some black, shaken
hill and slipping, lurching
on a viscous something most like blood

that trickles down its side.
Until that awful, death-dark
moment when one step returns in
finding nothing where it should have marked
a way; but nothing there except a wide

uncharted gap. There I fall
and drop disgusted (no, much more—
done) down and breathe, I think, my last.
Finished, flickering, almost out—but then, before
the final rattle, something still and small.

All dead, but new-found ears that hear!
No life, but past-blind eyes that see!
It's true, the rumors live again.
I'm hugged and laughed with, told with awful
tenderness that he has long been
on his way to me.

The Lion and the Lamb

Often at night, in the long harsh slide from
wakefulness to sleep, the same vision would appear—
he would see himself walking alone on a vast savannah,
void of all others, naked in a twilight of shadows
and rasping breezes, blowing hot and cold.
He would furtively slink along
in that glaring emptiness, moving in quick jerky
fear of something at first unknown—but then a frantic
    dash
as far behind deep in the distance
a tawny, bobbing spot took shape as a four-legged beast
in full charge. He would run madly with no goal
as the lion bounded nearer, the last glint of day
reflecting golden and fearsome off the full-maned face,
the beast's awful growling would draw closer and
his last frantic cries for help
and his last mad casting about for
what he built into his life
would be in vain, and the lion would bound closer
and roar once, roar twice
and reach to smash him irrevocably down
as he'd toss and groan to sleep.
Often before dawn, in the gentle rise from sleep,
he would glimpse a space, softly lit,
with a squat device of stones
upon which a lamb, all white and silent, lay bleeding
    and dead,
and friends running up and weeping with him.
He is stunned and looks long at
the monarch who has turned the sword from his breast
to slay the helpless beast,
and full of love for the lamb and fearless fear of the king.

Finally, one day around noon with
(he would later recall) a splitting headache
and the nag of still unfinished business to do—
his mind the tangled thread of a seemingly endless
        skein—
he heard as if a voice distinctly said:
"I am the lion pursuing you, and I am the lamb who
        died for you;
rest, dear child, for the lamb is the lion
and the lion is the lamb."

The Sensitive Nostrils of God

The kingdom smell is acrid rot
assumed in pre-romantic time of
sweating strife against the hells
on earth, within; contagion from adulterous love
unstoned; the viscous, clinging smell the Samaritan
could not for days wash off his hands.

The charnel smell of flesh
insinuates itself into the kingdom's air
like swamp breath blown from putrefying mud;
and over all the reek
of dried, opaquely blackened blood,
the flies upon it thick as matted hair
upon the baited bear.

Thus darkly does the kingdom smell
and to the Lord God Sabaoth so very fine
as full overpowers the fragrance from tables
laid over with damask, ambrosia, and wine.

Snow

The snow floats down, fluffing the city to death.
Children and those at peace like sails
catch the surge, mastered giggle-like, and roll
into the snow across the wide, wide spaces
white; the wraith—lovely, inscrutable—calls.
Cars begin to sputter and curse; one by one
withered white they die
as buttoned, capped, and booted, you and I
go dancing, tromping, dancing by.

Scots' Form in the Suburbs

The sedentary Presbyterians
awoke, arose, and filed to tables spread
with white, to humble bits that showed how God
Almighty had decided to embrace
humanity, and why these clean, well-fed,
well-dressed suburbanites might need his grace.

> The pious cruel, the petty gossipers
> and callous climbers on the make, the wives
> with icy tongues and husbands with their hearts
> of stone, the ones who battle drink and do
> not always win, the power lawyers mute
> before this awful bar of mercy, boys
> uncertain of themselves and girls not sure
> of where they fit, the poor and rich hemmed in
> alike by cash, physicians waiting to
> be healed, two women side by side—the one
> with unrequited longing for a child,
> the other terrified by signs within
> of life, the saintly weary weary in
> pursuit of good, the academics (soft
> and cosseted) who posture with their words,

the travelers coming home from chasing wealth
or power or wantonness, the mothers choked
by dual duties, parents nearly crushed
by children died or lost, and some
with cancer-ridden bodies, some with spikes
of pain in chest or back or knee or mind
or heart. They come, O Christ, they come to you.

They came, they sat, they listened to the words,
"for you my body broken." Then they ate
and turned away—the spent unspent, the dead
recalled, a hint of color on the psychic
cheek—from tables groaning under weight
of tiny cups and little crumbs of bread.

At the Sacrament, Late January in Chicago

The first pair "took and ate" and frost
welled up within the human soul.
The sorry sun, caloric lost,
glowed bleak-black, speechless in the cold.

No fire could break that grip. Ice lost
no hold until a ghastly heat
from steaming blood, a Word criss-crossed
pronounced a second "take and eat."

The Domestic Round

for her birthday in almost Spring

good loving you give me, the sun and the moon
are you, endpoints describing the empty
of me, a blindness before you so soon
that is light, a circle that frees
me for you
                 in the towns and the streets
the horses are edging their bodies around
to the season of mystery heats,
make pied and practiced pasture-ground
bed, while at night (in pale globular
phosphorescence) dancing and showing heels
what after all stars really are;
overhead the moon revives and reels
out her lunatics
                 preserving day, flashing night! you give
light to me, chances for reasons to live.

A Mother Muses on Receiving
the Kingdom of Heaven as a Child

Before he dove into the ice-clogged Mississippi
late on a chill Twin Cities night,
undone by self-doubt, booze, and frothy adulation,
John Berryman, the poet, only months before
this dark escape
had felt the quickening touch of grace
("let men consider
the steadfast love of the Lord")
and told us how it came about:
"Sucking, clinging, following, crying, smiling,
I come Your child to You."

Before the Lord began to fill our quiver
with the arrows of his blessing,
I thought the poet fuddled, frenzied, straining way too hard.
But now, behold my newborn babe:
　　she bawls, she stiffens spine,
　　rebuffs my love and softness,
　　and spits up most of my own milk.
She doesn't need theology, she knows by right of birth:
there is no tenderness to receiving the kingdom of heaven as
　　a child,
nothing demure, no pastel pinks or baby blues.
It is a test of strength, of will without a superego,
thrashing, howling furiously, suffused with self—
but then, sweet mercy,
overcome by restless hunger,
clinging, clinging, clinging utterly to me.

A Hymn to Marriage, Plena Gratia,
after Ten Years,
December 27, 1979

This poem belongs to her, for whom—
and for a lamp unlit one decade past—
I gave the well-known dimness of myself.
Wry lamp, when lit, to cast
a brighter light through ever deeper gloom.

I thought to wed would put the world in place.
But cares cascading down from God
knows where have filled our marriage full. Odd sound,
this great cacophony, to hide the note of grace
which Christ, whose whisper monks have vainly sought,
sings clear. The Friend of Children knows the embrace
of clutter, Word made man, leads to a kiss of life.

I thought to wed would pacify the flesh.
But marching, marching on goes lust,
dear foe. Strange gift of God this appetite
that leads through such dark night
before emerging to the sunlight of
the womb. What grace has wrought! to bloom this heat
into the flower of father-love.

I thought to wed would somehow twit Old Nick,
But little did I know the abscesses
of self that close encounters open wide.
Great illness—mine was fatal—needs a Great
Physician. Droll this grace to with this mate
increase my joy by pain, to with this bride
take me, diseased in soul, toward health.

"But the Lord Was Not in the Wind"
(1 Kings 19:11)

(My world, a crabbed war zone of oddities,
is all atwitter over women priests—
or "ministers" where this hat hangs. Fat feasts
it means for publishers, crisscrossing t's
and overloading i's. Once more a boisterous
fashion shouts aside the still small voice.)

    The Dutch doors of my mother's life
    are swinging shut. Below
    there lingers only dusk, above
    still shows a gentle light
    which seems—the mind's eye waked—to grow
    as darkness dims to night.

    My wife, my Martha, hardly stops
    when stopped, her mind is care-
    filled: children, plans, details of things
    just done, half done, to do.
    Ten years it took, sharp pain, despair,
    to see she's Mary too.

    My first-grade daughter is a frame
    roughed out—long months to fill
    the vacant arches of her jaw,
    short years to build her right.
    She calls great toil from me, whose skill
    at carpentry is slight.

Advent Journey to a Recent Widower

The road was hard, as the pain in her face
drove the smile from his eyes. Even grandchildren knew
that their friend would not hold them again in her arms.
And when death settled in
      like fog, did light break through? Did any hand
      reach out to him who'd not hold her again?

The road goes on, as the dying continues
as regular as seasons, or stars in their course,
in a round without end. And no mourners could sing
for themselves or the mourned
      if once a road had not begun somewhere
      and come at last to rest in Bethlehem—

The road was cold, and the fear in her face
was a spur to their feet through the fog-burdened night.
They were children of Promise whose eyes were yet dim
in the darkness of doubt.
      And then angelic voices pealed, the shepherds
      stared, the threshold's crossed, the star stood still.

The road is long, as the fear and the fog
turn their hearts into ice, and the children are cross
in the dark at their back. But the strain in their eyes
and the ache in their mind
      drain off as lights flick on and, now alone,
      the old man waits with open arms in the door.

Evensong, King's College Chapel

The child is three and wriggles constantly;
he doesn't care that at a king's command
these walls of passion-chiseled stone, cut clean
by filaments of light, arose. To him
these singers clothed in white are not the heirs
of other boys who stretch back to the verge
of time but kids just like his brother—songs
his brother sings he doesn't listen to,
so why now these? The liturgy as fine
as lace but supplements his litany,
"I gotta go." The man who struggles with
the wriggling child is forty-one, so thinks
he ought to find a symbol here,
perhaps the human race whom psalms (a mark
of general restlessness for God) as strong
and pure as honeycomb do not impress,
whom carvings aged and subtle (emblems of
Creator's loving skill) do not inspire,
and colors sharp and muted, glowing low
with mingled harmonies (in pictures of
the Savior's blood and pasture green) do not
entrance. But if the world is such a place,
and more, and music of this sort is like
the voice of God, he wonders why his heart
so often hardens to the melody
and takes no notice of the glory he
had helped create to wriggle as a three
year old at evensong within his arms.

Memorial Quartet
Francis A. Noll, November 6, 1918–January 6, 1993
(to my own son David)

(1)

At Calvary Baptist there has always been
a men's quartet, and so there was the night
of January ninth when once again
above the flood of words a song took flight
of faith from Henry, Terry, Wayne, and Dale.
Then high and fine Luane sang tenderly
to ask if souls were well when in a gale
the sorrows rolled like billows of the sea.

And now, months past, if still the sorrows roll
despite what we believe about the sting
of death, it must be for the gaping hole
he left who, even if his ear *was* tin,
so loved to hear the men of Calvary sing
their songs of Jesus' triumph over sin.

(2) Clearing out the Condominium

His birth took place election night and in
the week the European fighting ceased;
it ended just before the dreaded Clinton
age began. Between he farmed, then pieced
together education 'round a war
with ninety missions off a carrier,

and later walked with missionaries on ground
that from a lead Avenger he had bombed.

Yet of his worlds, Depression scarcity
(when Christmas meant an orange and maybe one
new shirt) had marked him deepest; otherwise
why find this master of philanthropy
with closet stuffed and bureau overrun
with slacks, socks, shoes, and bushels full of ties?

(3) Closing the Book

With scholar's scrawl I try to wrap it up—
where every number in this thick black book
meant both a shipment and another cup
of coffee with another friend across the state
of Iowa for over thirty years
(on visits home I often had a look
to see how "we" were doing).

                        Columns straight
were also strong—enough to banish fears
of want in points around the globe, and build
three homes, equip them with computers, dolls,
straight teeth, and calm the dark unknowns that filled
their rooms.

            But at the end the digits creep
where once they strode. I slowly sum the paltry
year-to-date and close the book and weep.

(4)

Will I ever hear a ball bounce on
a hardwood floor and not look up to seek
his face (and half expect to hear him give
the ref what for); or beat a frozen dawn
awake and silently steal down the stairs
and not in shadows think to catch a peak
of back bent over books as he prepares
for next week's class at Sunday School; or live
to see a child in church claw at his itching
tie and not remember our old strife;
or ever, to the last time I commit
a message to a child of mine, forget
the words—"I love you very much"—with which
he signed his letters, and defined his life?

For Mary, on Graduating from College

"And the dove came in to him in the evening;
and, lo, in her mouth was an olive leaf pluckt off." (Genesis 8:11)

At Noah's shoulder no doubt stood
his wife to share his longing for
the dove's return. She would
have felt the stab of grief before
he did, I'm sure, as he the good
news of the leaf cried out. A floor

or two below were sons. Next week
he'd loose the dove again: its beak
accomplished, now prepared for bleak
terrain, no need again their hands to seek.

Texts/Sermons

Advent Meditation on Psalm 119:25, 28, 31

"*My Soul Cleaves to the Dust*"
Did Mary tremble as her labor came
upon her, did her soul cleave to the dust?
What doubts about the angels' voices, doubts
about her sanity, her chastity,
left her distraught, afraid, unstrung, nonplussed?

And we, to whom no angels speak, who cleave
with passion to refined suburban dust,
what words could ever deconstruct the love
of wealth and power, what voice dispel our new
found certainties of gain and self and lust?

"*Strengthen Me According to Thy Word*"
What words, I want to know, could wrench the
    hold
of self, could raise us from the frantic dust
of aimless angst, could free us from ennui?
What word could reach a people sodden with
a flood of talk and spark a flame of trust?

One song was once enough to drive a herd
of shepherds joyfully before a gust
of heaven's glory, angelic voice enough
to warm their leaden hearts, enough to raise
those outcast souls, worth nothing, from the dust.

"I Cleave to Thy Testimonies"
But angels, I have said, do not discourse
with us. We're socialized into distrust
of words—by lies we view, by lies we're told,
and most of all by lies we tell ourselves
to prettify our lives of dust.

An infant's patient voice responds, a voice
of almost silent testament: "Entrust
yourselves to me. An angel I am not.
My word is lowly: cleave to me because
for you I cleave with passion to the dust."

Behold, I Stand at the Door

"Behold, I stand at the door, and knock: if any man hear my voice,
and open the door, I will come in to him and will sup
with him, and he with me." (Revelation 3:20)

An obscure artist threw his vision
of the knocking Lord on canvas once
and mocked
the King of Glory, Judah's Lion,
the Lord God Sabaoth
whose sword rests lightly in its sheath of grace.

Who is this wan Victorian,
this inoffensive rap-tap-tapping,
this massive, impregnable door,
this viny garden choking earth and walls?

Art need not lie: Charles Wesley
sang the chain-snapping gleam of his eye
and John Donne knew that nothing else matters
when that One stands at the heart and batters.

(The picture is Holman Hunt's *The Light of the World*, 1854.)

The Storm

*"And they feared exceedingly, and said one to another,
What manner of man is this, that even the wind
and the sea obey him?"(Mark 4:41)*

The storm arose with lightning force.
The heavens raged. The deep
Yawned black and wide to suck them down—
But Jesus was asleep.

"O Master, rise," they pled with him.
"Our boat is lost. And we
Are dead men staring at our doom"—
As violent rolled the sea.

Then Jesus stirred. He gazed at them
with care-worn eyes. "Who led
You to this boat to cross this lake?"—
And slowly sank their dread.

He turned to face the turbulence,
And spoke the Word. The shrill
Destroying blast, the storm, was done—
Both men and sea were still.

O faith, take heart! Be nerved with hope!
Do not despair! You pray
To one whose ear is keen, who speaks—
And winds and waves obey.

Meditation for a Christmas Communion, 1976

"How much more shall the blood of Christ . . . purge your conscience
from dead works to serve the living God?" (Hebrews 9:14)

I

"As often as you drink this cup"—
this galling sewer system of the flesh?
this putrefying, blackened bowl of gore?—
you lay aside pretense, you join the real world,
you ask to learn no more.

You know enough:
the blood-thick tears a parent squeezes out
when told a child's genetic code is scrambled
like a jigsaw carved from ice;

the smallish bloody pulp
that fled the womb in haste, full months before
its time, that in hearts smashed a door
of hope that never can be shut again;

the cancers killing off young men,
the good ones, riding wild along the body's streams,
borne by blood to every corner of the human globe,
robbing them, robbing wives and children,
robbing homes and churches of what might have been;

the bad blood, most of all, that broods
within, that pulls us back into our selves,
that pours itself as sacrifice
upon no altar but the self-stuck self.

"As often as you drink this cup"?
So far a hell of a holiday this—
"You do remember me."

II

Remember: a fourteen-year issue of blood
dried up, sent back into its proper banks,
returned into an old one's vanquished arteries,
calmed by him who calmed the sea.

His birth itself was no doubt bloody
with only cold to cauterize,
with nosing shepherds crude and ruddy
offering eager awe but little else.

Peer deep into that blood-black hole,
the purest night of all,
tear face along that harsh wood,
imagine (if you can) the royal platelets,
bruised by spikes, now gushing forth,
embrace the cross.

III

The blood flows on: the foul and cleansing,
pure and putrid intermingling. In Christ
the bad blood doesn't disappear—not yet.
But good blood seeps across it (unbent children,
Kingdom coming, dulcet friendships,
faithful spouses, Rehabilitation under way).

Hail bright and dawning light!
Hail dayspring from on high!
Mystic mingling deep inside the virgin's womb,
"God's blood" flowing from "God's wounds,"
pure white lilies gathered round a gutted tomb.

Philippian Jailer

"What must I do to be saved?"(Acts 16:30)

The chains fell:
fell for chains to fall
within the cell
for him who outside guards the wall.
Chains in confusion falling wrong
savored *him* as they sprung
to the magic in the strangers' song.

—called back from dagger's slake
—slunk in, sweating palms and brow
—intimated on *his* arms, *his* legs, *his* back
the wrinkled chains lying black
upon the floor like snakes
—begging how can I escape?

Once again they fell:
almost dying to stay free of iron chains
others, hidden,
fell in unexpected answer
to his plea.

Friends

Lament from Ely Cathedral for
Sheri Nystrom Scandrett, 1966–1988

With wonderment our eyes were fixed upon
the past when—brrring! brrring!—double knelling bells
recalled us from sarcophagi of kings
and queens, the relics of Armada, Orange
but bloodless glory of a Revolution,
stone cathedrals now themselves as old
as stone, to say that you, blond sprite with child
and promise great, were dead.

The sweet cornets of Purcell, calm clear notes
of Byrd, the surging melodies from Handel's
teeming brain, and Charles Wesley's Love
Divine All Loves Excelling—sung full-throated,
joyfully to strong and expert strings—
were overwhelmed beyond, it seemed, recall
by roar of sudden screeching tires.

Cathedrals gray without, stand now revealed
as gray within, the glass of carmine, green,
and indigo sends up a shield to light,
exploding into mocking shards that ring
your godly, pert, but lifeless head.

And so we silent stand before the cool
recess where every British church records
the dead from Ypres, Dunkirk, and the Somme—
communing there with hopes destroyed and hearts
unmade, and long to hear again a viol's
whispered solace, long with eyes made blind
by tears to see reach down and glow upon
those names one shaft of light transfigured red
by passing through a Savior's rosy heart.

Pastor Harvey Marks a Decade with His Congregation

"A good man was ther of religioun . . . a Persoun. . . .
But Cristes lore, and his apostles twelve,
He taughte, and first he folwed it him-selve."
                            —The Canterbury Tales

How shall we describe what you have been to us
     and we to you? Ten years should be
enough to offer hints, suggest a sketch
     that outlines something we can see.

Are we a high-strung orchestra which you
guide through its paces like Sir George, or do
we sound more like a young, rambunctious band
that's always out of tune, and you the hand
that holds us to a simple, steady beat?
Perhaps you are a pair of tired feet
and we a body gross and oddly sized.
Or might you be a heart well exercised
propelling fresh cleansed blood to every cell?
Are we despotic managers who yell
at you, our overburdened secretary,
or workers both intense and contrary
and you, the foreman, who must get it done?
The possibilities go on and on.
Are we the subjects of your kingly rule
or kings ourselves and you the royal fool?
Are you the patient keeper of a zoo

who feeds the bear, the apes, the kangaroo
and tries to keep their garbage out of sight?
A local demi-god whose might is right?
A general? Chairman of the board? A cop?
A coach? The DJ of our holy hop?

Why carry on? Years past shrewd Chaucer sowed
        the seed we reap tonight, the thought
of one who humbly tried to follow what
        in pulpit, class, and home he taught.

"How beautiful are the feet of those who bring
good news." (Romans 10:15, NIV)

The sheep who trail the shepherd with the blood
marks on his hands and feet may think they need
no other aid, no other one to feed
them, no one else to turn them from the flood
or gather them when lightning-black clouds scud
across the sky—no other eye can lead
them through the shadow, none beside succeed
in whitening wool from clinging, clinging mud.

Such sheep are almost always wrong when right
if they, with eyes for just the shepherd, fail
to see what gifts the shepherd can impart.
No gift is finer than the tender light
from other feet—though bruised and torn of nail
themselves—that point us to the shepherd's heart.

To Arthur Holmes, on His Retirement

The gardener toils in nearly Sunday clothes
because the work—though often muddy, cold,
unnoticed, lonely, crowded round by foes
of man and beast—is good; and seedlings hold
a promise, though long hid from sight, he knows
may still in unseen distant days unfold,
and yet unfold, while harvest-tide bestows
more pure delight than miner's hoarded gold.

On the seventh day the primal Gardener stayed
his patient hand, exchanging toil for rest;
and so may under-gardeners, though arrayed
in simple, human flesh, embrace with zest
the chance to set aside a well-worn spade
if they have worked by Sabbath joy possessed.

A Historian's History, 1939–1989
(for George Marsden)

At five there is no text or footnotes. War
may rage—with GIs swarming east in France
and tracers lighting up the Presby sky
in Philadelphia between the strong-
holds of Van Til and Clark—but fishing on
the broad flat river, watching for the train,
and steady hours in church are not yet stuff
for serried lines and trailing hooks of prose.

At fifteen, firmament of consciousness
has come between the viewer and the viewed.
The text and notes are clearly different things
and usually clear that, of the honored Dutch,
Van Til should be the text, Van Brocklin note;
that Ashburn, Ennis, and Konstanty fill
the bottom of the page beneath the tales
spun out by Stonehouse, Murray, and disputes
on which of Charles Wesley's suspect lines
to nudge a little closer to the norms
of Knox and Heidelberg. But other plots
have not yet found their proper place upon
the page—the mists of family heritage
(Hurrah for *Harrison?*), the melodies
behind the words, the daughters of French Creek.

At fifty, text now comes with sub-texts, notes
with notes themselves. And many things
are snugly in their place—a spacious note
for fundamentalists, a note that roams
from edge to edge for golf; above, a text
divided into transformation and
antithesis, while Southernness now needs
more space within the bibliography.
And yet, and yet . . . Enough remains that might
be text, or might be note, or even could
be key-stroked from the screen to lend suspense—
the lines, once handed on to you, now passed
to children, students, friends, how will they sound
in other accents, other ears; the themes
and players gone from sight but not from mind,
what role is left for them; the secrets of
the pages yet unturned, who knows them but
the one who knows all texts and notes and hearts?

Cold Dawn at the Shelter
(for Alva Steffler)

Last Christmastide the angel came at six-
fifteen. While volunteers began to poke
the guests awake, collect the mats, and fix
the coffee for the breakfast line, the smoke
rose from first cigarettes, and one large man
groaned off the floor, breath harsh, a map of beet-
red lines high on his cheeks—he strains but can
not bend down far enough to reach his feet.

The angel teaches art design, his hair
is gray, he's fifty-odd. Straightway he goes
down on his knee, does not recoil from hot
dry skin, begins to tug one of a pair
of stained white socks around those death-puffed toes
and nonchalantly smiles and says "fear not."

Casting Christmas 1994

In memoriam:

David Oliphant, 22 October 1950–5 December 1994
Sanna Anderson Baker, 24 September 1949–20 September 1995

Now older, and often worn out when we hear
the stories from Matthew and Luke, I nod off,
and images fade from the clear-cut to soft
as sleep does some tricks with who's far and who's near.

And so I have seen on the screen of my mind
a face like Bill Clinton's decreeing that all
should pay a new tax, and an atheist friend
who aches to believe showing up at the crib
as one of the Magi come out of the East.

Myself? In a bed at the inn I am rolled
up tightly, distracted, but when in the deep
of night there arises commotion below,
I pray for a dart of compassion in cold
of soul before drifting again off to sleep.

The shepherds this year are the friends whom we see
on Sunday each week, with the faces of two
especially clear who have battled for life
and battled some more. When the angel proclaims
"Fear not," I see Sanna look up and speak first,
"Let us even now to Bethlehem go,"
and afterwards Dave is a shepherd who writes
the song mixing grief and rejoicing to guide
them all through the town to the hills and then home.

Big George

G. A. Rawlyk
19 May 1935 (Thorold, Ontario)–23 November 1995 (Ottawa, Ontario)

O Canada,
can you survive without George
Alexander Rawlyk there to fight the northern creep
of Yankee signals, sects, and selves?
Can any take his place to give the Yugoslav disease
its name? Will any still recall what dogged muscle
from Ukraine—with naught in hand and then *the*
　　　Crash—
once pulled with steady will from gritty mill?
Who stands on guard for you?

O George,
Rocky Mountain of the North,
you were so craggy and so unexpected.
Slavophile ecumenicist, peasant intellectual,
Baptist socialist, terrifying teddy bear,
a Genghis Khan to start September seminars
become by May a Father Brown.
Why now? For us, whose hearts were just
as poised to crack as Canada?

O Jesus,
ravisher but also knitter up
of hearts, stir up our hope for Canada
the Good, receive our gratitude for this
Melchizedek, and in your mercy let
us pass along his "squeezerino," please.

O Canada. O George. O Jesus.

Times Past

Verba Verbumque: Hus at Constance

Where once the dulcet pierce of Czech
had ably wrecked a house of fear
and ignorance, I now am torn from earth
by Latin—wolfsbane, numbing ears
that once were stormed (as though
great faults when cracking under quakes
would speak) by echoes of rebirth.

As if by hearing vulgar words the Church
would madly lurch toward doom,
while bishops working dioceses like mines
guffawed in Latin over piles
of coin and made of churches tombs
where priests lisped Latin in the mass
and as they plied their concubines.

These wise men heard and whored my words
then drew their swords to flail the air
so impiously charged with Czech. Their grip
grew insecure. The people surely couldn't bear
to have the secrets out. "The Trinity
is under siege! Beware the wine, the bread!"
They also said my politics were faulty.

So now because I spoke the speech
of those I preached to, wanted them to learn
what mystic obfuscation blurred
and barred from eager ears, I burn
for peasants, burghers, lords who knew
no Latin, go where voices cease
in wordless peace within the Word.

Stalingrad:
Even a Soldier Is the City of God

Through the blackly darkened corridor
and out the stained and ragged gate
the flowing army spread
in pulsing rhythm marching from the dead;
its fiery banners banged headlong beside the way
till one was caught and fell,
blocking others backing up the strait.

With cries of disbelief
the street lamps turned and poured their light
upon the fleeing forces
growing ever blacker in their courses.
The dying city lurched,

it slowly turned—
in the brain a futile fumbling at the switches—
and fell to writhe upon the ground
and, as the tracers sucked once more the sky,
it died.

Martyrdom

(for the Rev. Robert Ziemer,
translator of the New Testament into Raday,
who was killed by the Viet Cong at Ban Me Thuout,
during the Tet offensive, January 31, 1968)

(1) The Lion

Trickling down from year to year
from a tawny, lacerated side
the river ministers to fears and Fear.

Some few chosen who have died
to guard the lion's blood
and spare his word
have mingled blood into the flood
and joined their bodies to the tide

that senses atrophied and blurred
may dip into this primal flow
and in the laving may be cured.

(2) The Dragon

Beside the banks the dragon stalked,
disdainful of the cooling stream
that drew the thirst-mad race
to realize its racial dream.

At first he'd pleading coax
with logic like a mace
to pander off his hoax
upon the dying race;

but when they wouldn't hear
he'd raise his colic ire
and with his mystic dragon might
he'd scourge them with his fire.

(3) The Warrior

Through duress night and day
he too strode along the stream
and calmly put off those
who called him, "Flee, away!"
He rose at dawn
and daylong called the thirsty drink
until the hosts of night
drove him from the river's brink.
At last one clouded day
the dragon came
to wreak his wrath
upon the warrior and the Name.
He stood, he fought
to tame the dragon's flaming cry
but soon he weakened and was thrown
into the long defended stream to die.

(4) The End and a Beginning

When his shed blood had vanished in the
    flood,
when he had taken his last breath,
in the Savior's gore was seen once more
the dazzling sheen of death.

In Rama Sat Rachel Weeping,
with Wilfred Her Husband

The German shard that pierced her Georgie's brain
made her a casualty as well. Poor Fred,
consistent Fred, was not at home when like
a beast encamping on its prey the car,
that olive drone of death, stopped at their curb.
"Good God," she wept, and clutched the major's arm,
"how did, oh for my life, how did he die?"

She never knew how she had reached the phone
or how she saw to dial. "He's gone, oh Fred,
he's gone. But Fred, praise God, the major says
he lost his life in peace, without delay,
as smooth and clean as once he mowed the grass."

At last the days took shape again, now past
the endless calls, the ersatz coffee and
the tears poured out like rivers with the friends
from Prince of Peace, the patient rummaging
of memories by Fred. And gradually,
through hours of gazing out above the stacks
of mail, she came to feel that she could bear
the strain of going on because her George
had not been forced to suffer as she had.

For several months in 1953
they took a turn at toddler care (the walls

were bright and signs proclaimed The Manger Room)
until a woman new at Prince of Peace
in thoughtless haste removed a squirming child
from Rachel's fumbling efforts with a pin
as if to say, "Here, this is how we do
it if we've had our own." Then once again
it fell to Fred, while coarse tears seared her face,
to carefully explain that they, years past,
had once a son whose life was lost at war.

Fred died in time, as calmly as he lived.
But Rachel lingered long, a withered face
behind the faded curtains and the star
whose tarnished points could still arrest the sun
on winter days. At last her time to leave
arrived, and she began to parcel out
her life one final time. She packed her Gold
Star uniform with care. She fondled all
the scraps that bore his memory, until
at last she turned to Wilfred's artifacts.

She almost missed it at the end because
it looked so like a piece of trash amid
Fred's ordered files, the outside twisted, stained
and streaked with gray. The shredding leaves inside
fell into pieces when she pulled them out.
Before she put the tatters side by side
and tried to puzzle out the words, she guessed

what he had hid and now she'd found within
this envelope from 1944.

"the fire across the squad . . . nowhere to go
but down . . . and George who caught it first . . . we tried
to get him back . . . pinned down . . . god-awful, raved
and raved . . . they cursed at us to shut him up
but it was only 9 a.m. . . . at night
we dragged him back . . . he tried . . . too much . . . for
        three
whole days . . . he never once lost consciousness . . .
we thought you and the missus ought to know."
She dropped her hands, the pieces fluttered down,
she crumpled nearly to the floor where eyes,
all reading past, yet still by grace could glimpse
the paper that had borne this second death.
The folds were worn clear through, the lines were
        smeared
and even washed away in patches, pulped
by just one pair of hands, two bleeding eyes.

She found the bed and sat and stared
out to the lawn he'd cut . . . they'd cut. All still
the hours passed. The German shard that pierced
her Wilfred's heart at last had lanced her wound.

Election 1968

There penciled in against the sky
stick men motionless,
angular Olympians pushing back the night;
as if their cold and practiced sight
could penetrate a madness
and reveal if now, today, we hear a speech
or watch the speaker die.

Mark A. Noll (Ph.D., Vanderbilt University) is McManis Professor of Christian Thought and professor of church history at Wheaton College. He is a leading church historian with many works to his credit, including *A History of Christianity in the United States and Canada*, *The Scandal of the Evangelical Mind*, and *Adding Cross to Crown: The Political Significance of Christ's Passion*.